GOD MADE THE
DINOSAURS

MICHAEL AND **CAROLINE CARROLL**

Illustrated by **JESÚS SOTÉS**

The **Faraday Institute** for Science and Religion

ZONDERkidz

This book is dedicated to Arthur Michael Carroll

ZONDERKIDZ

God Made the Dinosaurs
Copyright © 2023 by SPCK
Illustrations © 2022 by Jesús Sotés

Requests for information should be addressed to:
Zonderkidz, *3900 Sparks Dr. SE, Grand Rapids, Michigan 49546*

ISBN 978-0-310-14471-7 (softcover)
ISBN 978-0-310-15210-1 (audio download)

Any internet addresses (websites, blogs, etc.) and telephone numbers in this book are offered as a resource. They are not intended in any way to be or imply an endorsement by Zondervan, nor does Zondervan vouch for the content of these sites and numbers for the life of this book.

The views expressed in this book are those of the authors and contributors and may or may not be shared by others mentioned in the text. Every effort has been made to seek permission for images that have been used as reference for illustrations in this book.

Scripture quotations marked CEV are taken from the Contemporary English Version copyright © American Bible Society, 1991, 1992, 1995. Scripture quotations marked TLB are taken from The Living Bible © 1971.Used by permission of Tyndale House Publishers. Scripture quotations marked NET are taken from the NET Bible, New English Translation, and are copyright © 1996 by Biblical Studies Press, LLC. NET Bible is a registered trademark. Scripture quotations marked NIV are taken from The Holy Bible, New International Version. Copyright © 1979, 1984, 2011 by Biblica. Used by permission. All rights reserved. "NIV" is a registered trademark of Biblica. Scripture quotations marked NLT are taken from the Holy Bible, New Living Translation, copyright © 1996. Used by permission of Tyndale House Publishers, Inc., Carol Stream, Illinois 60189, USA. All rights reserved. Scripture quotations marked TEV are taken from The Good News Bible, The Bible in Today's English Version. New Testament © 1966, 1971, 1976 by the American Bible Society.

Image acknowledgements: Adobe Stock, pp. 14, 18, 23, 26, 40, 41, 45, 55; Getty Images, mottled texture, dinosaur tracks, pp. 7, 14, 18, 20, 21, 23, 24, 26, 28, 29, 34–5, 37, 40, 42, 44, 45, 50, 56; Bob Nichols, p. 28; Louise Psihoyos p. 41; Shutterstock, pp. 28, 37, 40; Velizar Sim, Julia Clarke and Chad Ellison, p. 43.

All listed ton weight measurements are based on the short/North American ton.

First published in Great Britain in 2022, Society for Promoting Christian Knowledge.

Zonderkidz is a trademark of Zondervan.

Zondervan titles may be purchased in bulk for educational, business, fundraising, or sales promotional use. For information, please email SpecialMarkets@Zondervan.com.

Interior Design: Mandy Norman

Printed in Korea

23 24 25 26 27 / SAM / 10 9 8 7 6 5 4 3 2 1

ABOUT THE FARADAY INSTITUTE FOR SCIENCE AND RELIGION

God Made the Dinosaurs was produced in collaboration with the Faraday Institute for Science and Religion, an interdisciplinary research and communication enterprise linked to the University of Cambridge. Steph Bryant, Lizzie Henderson, Cara Parrett, and Naomi Brehm, who contributed to this book, are all part of the Faraday Institute's Youth and Schools Team. They are committed to providing high-quality events and resources that encourage young people of all ages and backgrounds to explore their questions about the interactions between mainstream science and wholehearted religious faith in exciting and engaging ways.

If you and your children enjoy reading *God Made the Dinosaurs*, you can explore more about science, faiths, and the amazing things God has done at: www.faradaykids.com. You'll find activities, videos, age-specific answers to common big questions, as well as plenty of other resources.

Check out www.faradayeducators.com for information about resources and events for parents, teachers, and other educators.

This project and publication were made possible by the support of a grant from the John Templeton Foundation. The opinions expressed in this publication are those of the authors and do not necessarily reflect the views of the John Templeton Foundation.

CONTENTS

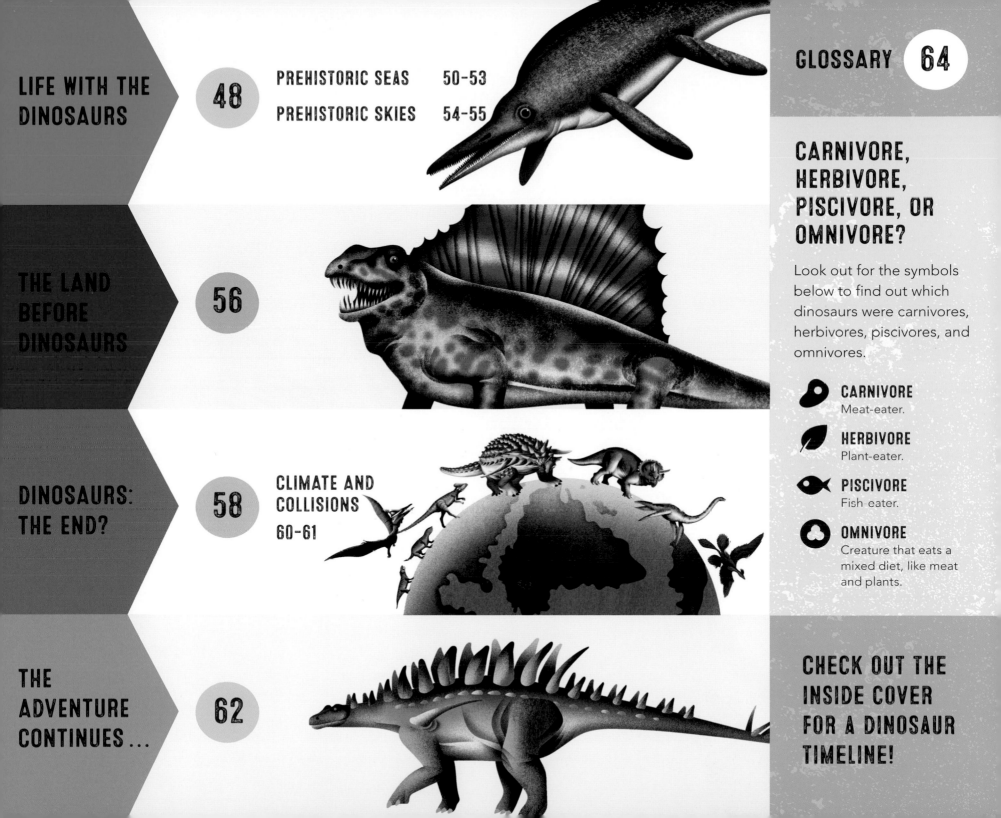

CARNIVORE, HERBIVORE, PISCIVORE, OR OMNIVORE?

Look out for the symbols below to find out which dinosaurs were carnivores, herbivores, piscivores, and omnivores.

CARNIVORE
Meat-eater.

HERBIVORE
Plant-eater.

PISCIVORE
Fish-eater.

OMNIVORE
Creature that eats a mixed diet, like meat and plants.

CHECK OUT THE INSIDE COVER FOR A DINOSAUR TIMELINE!

God's world has changed a lot during its long history. Continents have crashed together and split apart, oceans have opened and closed, and there have been millions and millions of different kinds of plants and animals.

Back when the dinosaurs roamed the Earth, the seas were full of great toothed reptiles chasing heavily armored fish, and the skies hosted huge flying reptiles, soaring like dragons among the clouds. But the land was ruled by dinosaurs of all different kinds, including the largest creatures ever to walk the Earth!

> The earth belongs to God! Everything in all the world is his!
> Psalm 24:1 TLB

MAGNIFICENT DINOSAURS, MAGNIFICENT GOD

These fascinating creatures were each crafted by God through the amazing processes he used to create the universe. They lived long, long ago, but their fossils (remains **preserved** in rocks) tell us lots about what the world was like long before humans existed. More than that, they tell us about God's power, love, patience, and great imagination. By exploring the natural world, we can learn about the awe-inspiring God who made it all.

He made tiny, speedy dinosaurs and colossal, lumbering ones. He made striped dinosaurs and others with feathers. He made spotted dinosaurs and some with crowns and horns. They all show off how imaginative God is!

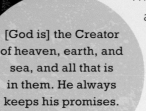

[God is] the Creator of heaven, earth, and sea, and all that is in them. He always keeps his promises.

Psalm 146:6 TLB

DINOSAURS AND THE BIBLE

The **Bible** teaches that God made and still looks after everything in the entire universe. But lots of interesting things we know about from science, from the **Big Bang** to koalas and kangaroos, aren't mentioned in the Bible, including dinosaurs (other than the birds, see p. 21). That's because the Bible wasn't written to be a science textbook or a list of things that God made.

WHAT'S THE BIBLE FOR?

The people who wrote the different parts of the Bible talked in many ways about God as the creator of the universe, but they focused on talking about *why* he created everything rather than *how* he created it. The Bible can help us explore our really big questions about who God is, who we are, as well as our place, meaning, and purpose in his incredible universe. Lots of Christians think science is a wonderful gift from God to help us to explore some of our other big questions about his universe, such as how he created everything.

DISCOVERING GOD'S DINOSAURS

People have been using science to learn about dinosaurs for a long time, but there are still many marvelous mysteries left to uncover. Bit by bit, science helps us add to our best understanding of how things work. As we explore, we sometimes find that things are different, more complicated, or more exciting than we thought. We are always discovering more about God's spectacular universe!

Planet Earth was formed about 4.6 billion years ago from space rocks crashing and squishing together as they zoomed around the sun. Scientists think that there's been life on Earth for about 3.6 billion years.

At first, all living things were tiny single-celled **organisms**, a bit like **bacteria**. But, gradually, an astonishing variety of life has developed—from huge, noisy, or colorful things to tiny, silent, or almost see-through ones. What an imaginative **creation**!

UNDERSTANDING EVOLUTION

Evolution means "change over time." Lots of people, including the famous Charles Darwin, have made discoveries that help us to think about how living things have gradually become more and more varied. We refer to our best current scientific ideas about this exciting process as the theory of evolution.

SMALL CHANGES

Change over time happens because every living thing is like its parents but also a little bit different from them. Sometimes, small changes that make a creature different from its parents can be very useful. They might help the creature get more food, hide from **predators**, or look more attractive to creatures of the same species. If they help the creature have more babies, then these changes are likely to be passed on to the next generation. Over many **generations**, lots of little changes add up to big differences, resulting in more and more new shapes, sizes, colors, and (eventually) new species.

ONE HUGE, COMPLICATED FAMILY!

To help us study God's huge family of living things, we divide it into different groups based on how closely related the living things are. All the creatures in one group are more closely related to each other than they are to anything outside that group.

SPECIES

The name we use for one of the smallest groups is "species." You could picture it like a leaf on the family tree. Species means a group of closely related living things that are similar enough to each other that they can have healthy babies together.

GENUS

The next biggest kind of group is called a "genus." This is a collection of closely related species that all have particular things in common—they sit together on the tree of life like leaves attached to the same twig.

In the case of *Tyrannosaurus rex* [ty-RAN-oh-SORE-us REX], *Tyrannosaurus* is the name of the genus it is part of and *rex* is its species name.

TREE OF LIFE

The dinosaur group contains thousands of different genus (and species) groups—like a big, leafy tree branch. The dinosaur group sits alongside other massive groups, such as mammals, insects, and amphibians. These sit together within an even bigger group—the animal kingdom. Even so, animals are still just one part of God's awe-inspiring tree of life.

So how did God make dinosaurs? Many Christians think God created every single weird and wonderful living thing through the processes of evolution. That includes the dinosaurs!

All over the world, scientists called paleontologists [PAY-lee-un-TOLL-uh-jists] dig up fossils and study them. Their discoveries show us lots of exciting things about the dinosaurs God has made, and we are always finding out more.

CAKE LAYERS

Deep down inside planet Earth, it is hot and squishy. But the Earth's surface is made of layers of rock arranged like the layers in a giant cake.

This "rock record" tells us about Earth's history. Each time period represented in the rocks has been given a name. Most of God's dinosaurs lived in a long time period called the Mesozoic [MES-oh-ZOE-ick] era, which can be divided into three shorter periods. The oldest of these is the Triassic [Try-AH-sick], next is the Jurassic [juh-RAH-sick] and the most recent is the Cretaceous [kre-TAY-shus], which ended about 66 million years ago. You might not be able to imagine that far back, but God was there, enjoying his dinosaurs roaming through the Mesozoic era.

He [Jesus] existed before anything else, and he holds all creation together.
Col. 1:17 NLT

CENOZOIC	QUATERNARY
	NEOGENE
	PALEOGENE
MESOZOIC	CRETACEOUS
	JURASSIC
	TRIASSIC
PALEOZOIC	PERMIAN
	CARBONIFEROUS
	DEVONIAN
	SILURIAN
	ORDOVICIAN
	CAMBRIAN

PRECAMBRIAN

HOW FOSSILS ARE MADE

Fossils are the remains or traces of creatures and plants that have turned to stone over thousands or millions of years. They can be found all over God's world.

Most fossils form when a creature dies and is buried quickly—sometimes in a landslide, a flood, or at the bottom of a lake. The soft, meaty parts of the creature's body usually rot away or are eaten by scavengers, but the hard parts remain. That's why we often find fossilized bones, teeth, shells, and claws. The creature's remains get buried deep underground by layers of mud and sand that gradually turn into sedimentary [SEH-deh-MEN-tuh-ree] rock through pressure and chemical changes. Over time, water dissolves the buried remains and

replaces them with minerals and rock crystals, creating a rock copy of the original remains—a fossil.

Certain conditions have created some very unusual fossils. In some cases, creatures have dried out like Egyptian mummies before being buried, so some of their skin and other soft parts are fossilized too. In other rare cases, some original remains have actually been preserved inside the rock. Finds like these mean that people such as Dr. Mary Schweitzer (see p. 33) can even explore what some of the squishy bits of God's long-ago dinosaurs were like!

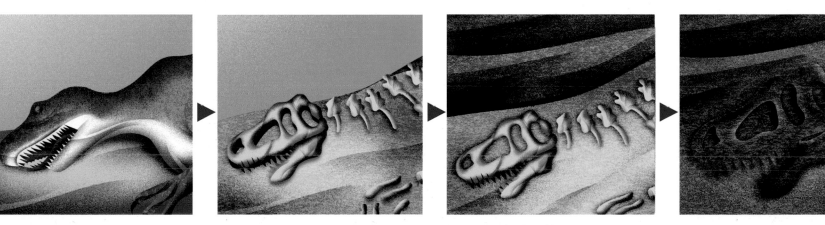

TRACE FOSSILS

Fossils can also be made from the marks that God's living things leave behind, like burrows, footprints, or poo (called "coprolites" [KOP-ro-lights]). These "trace fossils" can tell us about what these creatures ate, how they walked, how heavy they were, and even how they behaved.

LOOKING BACK IN TIME

Fossils are like a time machine, helping us learn about amazing creatures that lived long ago. One day you could be a paleontologist, studying fossils and the ancient life of God's creation!

FOLLOWING FOOTPRINTS

Some remarkable trace fossil discoveries have helped paleontologists learn more about God's ancient dinosaurs and the places where they lived.

"DINOSAUR ISLE"

Dinosaur fossils are found all around the world, even in Antarctica. But some places, such as Scotland's Isle of Skye (sometimes called "Dinosaur Isle"), seem to have been particularly good for making fossils.

In Mesozoic times, the island had warm, shallow seas, lagoons, and steamy fern forests. Many dinosaurs left behind traces like long lines of footprints (trackways) in the mud, and these very slowly turned to stone. These traces give us hints about the lives of God's dinosaurs, including some of the biggest to ever walk on Earth.

It's amazing that we can follow the footsteps of God's dinosaurs from millions of years ago.

DR. STEVE BRUSATTE

Dr. Steve Brusatte, a **Christian** and paleontologist at the University of Edinburgh, has always loved dinosaurs. He and other scientists found a big trackway on the Isle of Skye in an area that used to be a lagoon. These trace fossils were made by sauropods [SORE-uh-pods] (see p. 44)—huge, long-necked dinosaurs that were the size of two or three elephants. Can you picture them wading through the shallow lagoons of God's Jurassic period?

EDWARD HITCHCOCK

In America, in the 1800s, church **pastor** and **geologist** Edward Hitchcock was looking for new places to mine coal from the ground when he spotted thousands of unrecognizable footprints. Because of the shape of the tracks, he thought that they had been made by "flightless birds of a gigantic size." We now know that today's birds are living dinosaurs (see p. 21)! So Edward was closer to the truth than many realized.

TEXAS TRACKWAYS

Sometimes we can make funny mistakes when we try to learn more about God's world.

Texas has a long trackway of fossil footprints left by a herd of sauropods. Next to those footprints are smaller prints. Some of them look a bit like human footprints, so a few people wondered if huge dinosaurs had lived at the same time as people. Dr. Berney Neufeld, a Christian and geologist, wasn't sure. In 1975, he followed the tracks for many miles. The farther he went, the clearer the tracks became, showing footprints with only three toes, like small meat-eating dinosaurs, not human feet. There's no evidence that people and dinosaurs (apart from modern birds) ever lived at the same time.

DISCOVERIES IN HISTORY

People have been uncovering clues about God's dinosaurs for a long time. Often, they found them by simply being curious about the world!

MARY ANN'S MARVELOUS DISCOVERY

Mary Ann Mantell lived in the 1800s. She loved rocks—the way they lay in the ground, their interesting shapes, and the mysterious fossils they sometimes held. Her husband, Gideon, was a geologist (and a doctor) and shared Mary Ann's love of rocks.

One day, Mary Ann found several strangely shaped stones that looked like the flat teeth of a gigantic iguana. She didn't know it at the time, but she had discovered a dinosaur! When Gideon wrote about it, he named the dinosaur *Iguanodon* (meaning "iguana teeth").

Genus: IGUANODON
[ig-WAH-no-don]
Lived: early Cretaceous period
Length: up to 26 feet
Weight: up to 4.4 tons

PRAYER
Thank you, God, for paleontologists, geologists, and other scientists who help us understand more about your amazing world.

BRINGING DINOSAURS TO LIFE

In the 1850s, more and more dinosaur discoveries were being made. Many people were curious about these mysterious creatures and the history of God's creation.

NOSES OR THUMBS?

English sculptor Benjamin Waterhouse Hawkins made some life-sized dinosaur models, beginning with *Iguanodon*. In addition to the teeth found by Mary Ann, people had found *Iguanodon* leg bones and a mysterious horn. At first, they thought *Iguanodon* had a horned nose, so Benjamin's model looked a little like a rhinoceros. But other fossil discoveries meant paleontologists soon realized that these "horns" were actually *Iguanodon* thumb spikes.

Stories like these show us how tricky it can be to work out what the fossil clues are telling us about God's extraordinary creation. God knows everything about each creature he has made, but we still have so much to discover. **So it is important and exciting to keep asking questions and learning more.**

HOT OR COLD?

When people like Mary Ann found dinosaur bones, they were full of questions and ideas. Many wondered if dinosaurs were ancient lizards because some of their bones looked similar to those of modern lizards. Most reptiles (such as snakes and lizards) are cold-blooded—their bodies don't make heat and their temperature depends on the air around them.

Birds and mammals (like us) are different—our warm-blooded bodies make their own heat. Because dinosaurs were thought to be like lizards, people thought they were also cold-blooded. Since working out that birds are living dinosaurs, scientists now think that at least some dinosaurs were also warm-blooded, like us!

Isn't it wonderful how we can keep discovering more and adding to our understanding of God's incredible world?

PUTTING IT ALL TOGETHER

Paleontologists use fossils to piece together as much as they can about these ancient, mysterious parts of God's creation. Over the years, all sorts of clever people have managed to work out how some dinosaurs moved, what they ate, how they lived, and even what color they were and what sounds they made!

MEET BIG AL!

"Big Al" is the name given to a particular *Allosaurus* [AH-lo-SORE-us] fossil found in Wyoming. All we have are his fossilized bones—no skin, muscles, heart, or lungs—but the bones can give us clues about the rest of him. Let's see if we can put Big Al together to picture what he looked like when he roamed God's Earth.

1 SKELETON

Look at Big Al's skeleton. He has holes in his head! Two holes are for his eyes and two for nostrils. Others are for nerves and muscles, like those that powered his huge jaw.

How many fingers and toes does his skeleton have? Look at his leg bones. Do you think he ran on two feet or four?

Al had a rough life. His damaged ribs and vertebrae (back bones) were broken in a fight. His right foot had a swollen, infected toe, which might have made it hard for him to hunt.

2 GUTS AND ORGANS

Now let's add some flesh to Al's bones.

Like you, Al had eyes, a nose, a brain, lungs, kidneys, and a stomach and intestines to digest his food.

Al had big eyes, so he could probably hunt at night, and his brain was shaped a bit like a modern crocodile's brain. Alligators and crocodiles are only distant relatives of dinosaurs, but this similarity suggests that, like crocodiles, Al's brain might have had a small area for thinking, but huge areas for making sense of things that he could smell and see.

3 MUSCLES

The ridges and smooth places on bones give us clues about where muscles attached and even how strong they were. We can also get clues about ancient dinosaur muscles by comparing their bones to those of their modern **descendants** (birds) and more distant relatives, like alligators.

PRAYER

God, you created the muscles, organs, nerves, skin, skeleton—all the details of all these amazing creatures. You're so smart!

4 SKIN

Very little *Allosaurus* skin has been found, so we don't know exactly what Al's skin was like. But some other fossils might give us clues. Different types of dinosaurs seem to have had different colors and patterns—scientists have found dinosaur skin impressions showing wrinkles, feathers, and scales, with some arranged in stripes, circles, or spots. So Al's skin might have been smooth, bumpy, and covered with scales or even feathers. He could have had fancy patterns and been any color of the rainbow.

If you could create a dinosaur with God, what would it look like?

PUTTING IT ALL TOGETHER

COLORFUL CREATURES

It's very difficult for paleontologists to work out the colors of God's ancient dinosaurs because we have only found dinosaur skin in stony fossil form. Some scientists have suggested that ancient dinosaurs might have been dull-colored, like rhinos and elephants. Others think some were brightly colored, like lots of their modern bird relatives. Exciting new finds are helping us work out more.

GLOSSY GLIDER

Crow-sized *Microraptor* [MIKE-row-RAP-tore] has also given us some incredible color clues! This strange-looking glider had wing feathers on its arms and legs, and eyes so large that scientists used to think it might have used them to hunt at night.

More recently, **microscopic** remains of special cell parts (called melanosomes [meh-LAH-noh-zohms]) have shown that its feathers had a colorful, glossy shine, a bit like the blue-black feathers of a raven. Modern birds with shiny feathers like this aren't active at night, so we now think *Microraptor* probably hunted in the daytime—all because of color clues. Perhaps God's Mesozoic world was full of shiny dinosaurs gliding and darting around.

CLEVER CAMOUFLAGE

In 2011, paleontologists found the most well-preserved armored dinosaur fossil ever discovered—*Borealopelta* [BORE-ree-ul-oh-PEL-ta] (see p. 25). Studying this special **specimen's** armor plates, scientists have discovered that it was reddish-brown with a lighter belly. Just like animals today, these colors probably provided camouflage from predators.

DID YOU KNOW?

Like many animals today, some male dinosaurs may have been brightly colored to help them attract mates, while females may not have been so brightly colored or dramatic.

SPECTACULAR SOUNDS

We hear all sorts of noises in God's wonderful creation today—grunts, squawks, quacks, chirps, songs, and more. **Paleontologists may never be certain what sounds dinosaurs made, but most think that they *did* make noises.** The inner ear bones of different dinosaur species show that they had quite good hearing, so they probably made sounds to communicate. They might have called to warn of danger, locate family, or show off for mating, like animals do today.

Lambeosaurus

Brachylophosaurus

ANCIENT ORCHESTRA

Some dinosaurs, such as *Lambeosaurus* [LAM-bee-oh-SORE-us] and *Parasaurolophus* [PAH-ruh-sore-oh-LOAF-us] (see p. 36), had big crests on top of their heads that connected to the insides of their noses. Paleontologists think that they may have pushed air through these crests, a bit like a trumpet, to make deep bellowing or booming sounds.

PRAYER

God, you're such an imaginative creator. It must have been amazing to hear all those dinosaurs calling out. Thank you for making such an exciting, noisy creation!

Scientists are doing fantastic work piecing together clues about God's incredible dinosaurs. Are you ready to find out more about some of these extraordinary creatures?

BRACHY-CROAK!-OSAURUS

Brachylophosaurus [BRACK-ee-LOAF-oh-SORE-us] had a throat pouch. Perhaps it could croak like a frog!

Fossils provide important clues about how dinosaurs fit into God's big family of living things and how they were related to each other (see p. 9).

Through his clever evolutionary processes, God made lots of different dinosaurs. Scientists divide dinosaurs into two main groups: the saurischians [so-RI-skee-ans] and ornithischians [OR-nih-THIS-kee-ans].

> O LORD, what a variety of things you have made! In wisdom you have made them all. The earth is full of your creatures.
> Psalm 104:24 NLT

Apatosaurus

SAURISCHIANS

"Saurischians" means "lizard-hipped," but don't be fooled—lizards aren't dinosaurs.

The saurischian group includes the biggest dinosaurs ever discovered, such as the long-necked sauropods (see p. 44) *Apatosaurus* [app-AT-oh-SORE-us] and *Diplodocus* [dip-LOD-oak-us], as well as the meat-eating theropods [THER-uh-pods] (see p. 32) like *Deinonychus* [dye-NON-ee-kus] and *Tyrannosaurus rex* (nicknamed T. rex for short).

Diplodocus

Tyrannosaurus rex

Deinonychus

DINOSAUR DINNER

Amazingly, fossils can often show what God's ancient creatures ate. Some were carnivores (meat-eaters), some were herbivores (plant-eaters), some were piscivores (fish-eaters), and some were omnivores (they ate almost anything)! Wondering why God might create carnivores? See p. 41 to learn more.

Stegosaurus

ORNITHISCHIANS

"Ornithischians" means "bird-hipped." This is confusing too because modern birds are part of the "lizard-hipped" saurischian group! All the ornithischians we have discovered were plant-eaters, including the duck-billed *hadrosaurus* [HAD-ro-SORE-us] (see p. 36), spiky-tailed *Stegosaurus* [STEH-go-SORE-us] (see p. 22), and three-horned *Triceratops* [try-SER-uh-tops] (see p. 29).

Hadrosaurus

Triceratops

THE NAME GAME

Fossils found in the 1800s by geologists such as the **Reverend** William Buckland (see p. 30) and Mary Ann and Gideon Mantell (see p. 14) got anatomist Sir Richard Owen thinking. The fossil creatures were similar to each other but different from anything else he knew about, so he suggested a special new animal group called "Dinosauria"—Greek for "terrible (or "fearfully great") lizard." We still call them "dinosaurs," even though we know that they're not lizards and weren't all big or scary!

Many ancient creatures were given names that we now know don't describe them well, like ichthyosaurs [ICK-thee-oh-sores] (see p. 52), meaning "fish lizard." though they weren't fish or lizards (or dinosaurs!). These out-of-date names remind us that people have been exploring God's world for a long time, gradually learning more, and sometimes realizing that old ideas weren't quite right.

THE REVD WILLIAM BUCKLAND

GIDEON AND MARY ANN MANTELL

SIR RICHARD OWEN

LIVING DINOSAURS?

There are many dinosaurs that we only know from fossils, but one big group is still around—birds! Their closest fossil relatives were theropods, like *Velociraptor* [vel-OSS-ih-RAP-tore] and *Tyrannosaurus rex*, many of which had bird-like bones, lungs, feathers, and more. So when you next see a chicken, eagle, or penguin, remember that **the age of God's dinosaurs is far from over**.

DINOSAUR DEFENSE

Some of God's dinosaurs protected themselves using built-in armor! Fossils show us incredible examples of hoods, crowns, and spikes that shielded animals against predators like toothy T. rex and speedy *Velociraptor*.

STEGOSAURUS

With spectacular spikes and plates, *Stegosaurus* was a particularly famous armored dinosaur. Its name means "roofed lizard," so called because the large plates along its back look a bit like a roof. Scientists have had fun trying to understand the usefulness of these plates. Many think that they were useful for protection and keeping *Stegosaurus* cool (the same way an elephant's ears send warm blood near the skin's surface to cool it down). Maybe they helped it to show off or to attract mates? They may even have been able to change color!

Stegosaurus's tail also had a set of spikes, called a thagomizer [THAG-uh-my-zer], that it could swing like a club to scare or injure potential attackers. Each spike could be up to 3 feet long!

Genus: STEGOSAURUS
[STEH-go-SORE-us]
Lived: late Jurassic period
Length: up to 23 feet
Weight: up to 4.4 tons

PRAYER
Creator God, you deserve all our praise because you have made such magnificent creatures!

22

THE BONE WARS

In the 1870s, people were becoming fascinated by dinosaurs and fossils, and many wanted to be the first to make the next big discovery.

Two rival paleontologists, Edward Drinker Cope and Othniel Charles Marsh, heard rumors of giant dinosaur bones in the western USA and they rushed there to find the biggest, best, newest fossils. They found many new dinosaurs, but in their hurry to outdo each other, they used dynamite, probably destroying as many fossils as they found! One surviving dinosaur discovery was *Stegosaurus*, named by Marsh in 1877, but think what they could have unearthed if they'd been more careful.

This rivalry inspired a fossil-hunting period called the "Bone Wars" or "Great Dinosaur Rush."

STEGOSAURUS'S COUSINS

Stegosaurus had several close relatives called stegosaurs [STEH-go-sores]. This group of ornithischians show us more wonderful examples of God's creativity.

DACENTRURUS ▶
[DAH-cen-TROO-rus] had thin plates along its back and spikes along its tail.

MIRAGAIA ▶
[mi-ra-GUY-ya] had a long, graceful neck and small plates.

KENTROSAURUS ◀
[KEN-tro-SORE-us] had a long spike poking out of each shoulder.

HUAYANGOSAURUS ◀
[HWAH-yan-go-SORE-us] had plates shaped like spikes all along its back.

GIGANTSPINOSAURUS ▶
[JY-gant-SPY-no-SORE-us] had small plates but very large blades on its shoulders.

23

ANKYLOSAURUS

Ankylosaurus had some serious armor! If dinosaurs played sports, *Ankylosaurus* would have been a star football player. This ornithischian had horns and spikes on its head, tough scales—called scutes [skoots]—shielding its back and legs, and two protective collars of plates on its neck. Like *Stegosaurus*, its tail included a weapon (a bony club) it could swing to protect itself. **Isn't it incredible that God's creative processes bring about creatures that grow their own armor?**

Despite looking fierce with amazing armor and a giant body, *Ankylosaurus* didn't spend its time chasing other dinosaurs. It was a herbivore, with a large, parrot-like beak and tiny, leaf-shaped teeth, which were excellent for chewing plants.

Genus: ANKYLOSAURUS
[AN-key-low-SORE-us]
Lived: late Cretaceous period
Length: up to 26 feet
Weight: up to 7 tons

A VERY RARE FIND

An unexpected discovery introduced us to another of God's creatures, a close relative of *Ankylosaurus*.

In 2011, mine worker Shawn Funk was digging away on a hillside in Alberta, Canada, when he noticed something unusual. Scientists came and unearthed a remarkably well-preserved dinosaur fossil that not only had bones but also skin, muscle, and scales, all turned to stone. The dinosaur was named *Borealopelta markmitchelli* [BORE-ree-UL-oh-PEL-ta MARK-mitch-EL-ee], after the man who carefully dug the fossil out of the rock.

BOREALOPELTA

The special *Borealopelta* fossil is one of the most lifelike dinosaur fossils ever found. While some other dinosaur fossils show signs of skin or muscles, such as Leonardo the hadrosaur [HAD-ro-sore] (see p. 37), these specimens usually dry out and shrivel up before turning to stone, or are squashed during fossilization. This *Borealopelta* fossil kept its full shape.

It seems to have sunk upside down into sea floor mud. Scientists have been able to study the armored scales, plates, skin, and even the ground-up plants in its stomach in more detail than ever before. **There are still questions to be answered but, yet again, God's astonishing processes of fossilization help us glimpse the distant history of his beautiful creation.**

Extraordinary fossils like this show us more than we ever thought we would discover about God's dinosaurs!

Genus: BOREALOPELTA
[BORE-ree-UL-oh-PEL-ta]
Lived: early Cretaceous period
Length: up to 18 feet
Weight: up to 1.4 tons

DINOSAUR DEFENSE

We still have so much to uncover about God's wonderful dinosaurs! Some are still quite a puzzle.

PACHYCEPHALOSAURUS

We have very few complete fossil *Pachycephalosaurus* skeletons, and scientists have lots of questions about them.

PRAYER

God, thank you that your world is so complex and beautiful—more than we could ever imagine! Please help us discover even more about your astonishing creation.

MYSTERIOUS TEETH

Differently shaped teeth help animals eat different things. Many carnivores have sharp, pointed teeth; piscivores often have lots of little spiky teeth; while herbivores generally have teeth that can cut and grind tough plants. *Pachycephalosaurus* seems to have pointy teeth in the front top jaw and cutting, grinding teeth at the sides. Scientists think that this ornithischian dinosaur ate a varied diet of leaves, nuts, fruits, and maybe meat too.

Stygimoloch

Dracorex

MYSTERIOUS HEAD

Pachycephalosaurus had a big head with a thick dome at the top of its skull. Many scientists agree that the domes were probably used when fighting, but they disagree on whether rivals would have crashed their heads together or head-butted other parts of their rival's body.

Genus: PACHYCEPHALOSAURUS
[PACK-key-SEFF-uh-low-SORE-us]
Lived: late Cretaceous period
Length: up to 16 feet
Weight: up to 992 pounds

Pachycephalosaurus

Great is our Lord and mighty in power; his understanding has no limit.
Psalm 147:5 NIV

SAME OR DIFFERENT?

Over the years, paleontologists have identified what seemed to be different types of pachycephalosaur. They thought that *Dracorex* [DRAY-ko-rex] and *Stygimoloch* [stih-jee-MOE-lock] were close relatives of *Pachycephalosaurus*, but with differently shaped skulls.

More recently, paleontologists Jack Horner and Dr. Mark Goodwin suggested that *Dracorex* and *Stygimoloch* might be young *Pachycephalosaurus* (see Dr. Peter Dodson's similar discovery about hadrosaurs, p. 36). They think that the differently sized fossils, spikes, horns, and head domes show *Pachycephalosaurus* at different ages. New fossil finds seem to support this idea, and the more we discover, the better we'll understand these fantastic creatures!

AN ADVENTURE OF DISCOVERY

Paleontology is full of fun mysteries, and scientists work hard to think of creative ways to best understand what is found. We may never understand everything about God's spectacularly huge and detailed universe, but we do know that he loves it when we explore his creation. The Bible tells us that God loves us and wants to be our friend, sharing in all we do. **So we can see science as an exciting adventure of discovery alongside the God who made it all.**

BEAKS, HORNS, AND FRILLS

Another exciting and diverse group of God's ornithischian dinosaurs are the ceratopsians [SER-uh-TAHP-see-uns]. From small, early examples to the enormous *Triceratops* that lived later, their fossils give us big clues about how the group developed through the generations.

PSITTACOSAURUS

Psittacosaurus, an early ceratopsian, didn't really have a frill or horns, but it did have a large beak like other ceratopsians and cheek spikes. Hundreds of *Psittacosaurus* fossils have been found—from babies to fully grown adults. There are so many that they are called the sheep of the Mesozoic.

Genus: PSITTACOSAURUS
[SIT-uh-kuh-SORE-us]
Lived: early Cretaceous period
Length: up to 6.5 feet
Weight: up to 44 pounds

PROTOCERATOPS

Protoceratops was an early ceratopsian dinosaur living in the late Cretaceous period. It was the size of a large dog, with a beak and wide neck frill but, unlike later ceratopsians, it had spikes instead of horns.

Genus: PROTOCERATOPS
[PRO-toe-SER-uh-tops]
Lived: late Cretaceous period
Length: up to 8 feet
Weight: up to 386 pounds

DR. PETER DODSON

Dr. Peter Dodson is an expert on dinosaurs, especially the ceratopsians. He helped discover one, *Avaceratops* [AY-vuh-SER-uh-tops], in Montana back in 1981, and even named a dinosaur found in China *Auroraceratops* [or-OR-a-SER-uh-tops] (in Latin, "dawn horned face") after his wife, Dawn. Dr. Dodson loves the diversity of dinosaurs and, as a Christian, believes them to be the "jewels of God's creation."

28

LIAOCERATOPS

Liaoceratops, another early ceratopsian, was also found in the rich fossil beds of Liaoning Province, China.

It seems to be the earliest known member of the family group that includes the famous *Triceratops*, which lived later in the Cretaceous period.

Genus: LIAOCERATOPS
[lee-ow-SEH-ruh-tops]
Lived: early Cretaceous period
Length: up to 3 feet
Weight: up to 4.4 pounds

PRAYER

Creator God, you must be so big and powerful to have made all these astonishing dinosaurs. Thank you for such an incredible part of your creation. Each one shows me how wonderful you are.

TRICERATOPS

Triceratops was much bigger than earlier ceratopsian dinosaurs, much stronger, and much more spectacular too! *Triceratops* had three horns—two arranged like bull horns and one on its nose, like a rhinoceros. The horns could have been used to fend off attacks, to fight other *Triceratops*, or to attract females.

Genus: TRICERATOPS
[tri-SEH-ruh-tops]
Lived: late Cretaceous period
Length: up to 26 feet
Weight: 6.7 tons

BIG TEETH, BIG ATTITUDE?

THE REVEREND WILLIAM'S "MEGA" DISCOVERY

Around the 1800s, many church ministers enjoyed exploring the natural world, excited to learn more about God's creation. The Reverend William Buckland, a **minister** in England, collected and studied lots of fossil bones. In 1824, he named a recent discovery *Megalosaurus*, meaning "great lizard." This was the first dinosaur to be given an official name—even before the word dinosaur had been invented (see p. 21)! William Buckland's careful ways of studying fossils helped shape modern paleontology.

FUN FACT

Apparently, William Buckland used to fall asleep while riding his horse. But the story goes that the horse was so used to stopping at interesting rocks, when it came across some, it would snort to wake William up!

Genus: MEGALOSAURUS
[MEG-uh-low-SORE-us]
Lived: mid-Jurassic period
Length: 36 feet
Weight: up to 3.3 tons

ROCK LAYER TIME MACHINE

William Buckland noticed that there were many rock layers, each containing different fossils that didn't look like any animals alive in his day. He worked out that a long time had passed since God first made the creatures he saw far down in the rocks. He called the rock layers "God's steps of creation."

Genus: DILOPHOSAURUS
[die-LAHF-uh-SORE-us]
Lived: early Jurassic period
Length: up to 23 feet
Weight: up to 1,246 pounds

DILOPHOSAURUS

Dilophosaurus was light for its size and built for running and jumping, using its powerful back legs and kangaroo-like tail for balance. This speedy theropod had long, clawed fingers and many small, serrated teeth. Trackways believed to have been made by its close relatives seem to show feather imprints where the creature rested on the ground, so it might even have been feathery! It's so exciting that we can collect and understand different kinds of evidence to build a picture of God's creatures from long ago.

> The LORD made the earth by his power; by his wisdom he created the world and stretched out the heavens.
> Jeremiah 10:12
> TLB

COELOPHYSIS

Coelophysis is a much smaller, lighter cousin of *Dilophosaurus*. With a mouth full of needle-like teeth and large, forward-facing eyes like the eyes of an eagle, scientists think that it was another speedy little hunter.

A whole pile of these little dinosaurs were found fossilized together in a desert in New Mexico. They seem to have been killed by a flash flood, similar to those that still sometimes splash through the canyons, burying everything in their path. Although it can be sad to think about animals dying, fossils from natural events such as this can freeze a moment in time. They give us clues about things, such as which animals lived together in the same area at the same time.

Genus: COELOPHYSIS
[SEE-lo-FY-sis]
Lived: late Triassic period
Length: up to 11.5 feet
Weight: up to 66 pounds

THEROPODS

All the carnivorous dinosaurs we know about belong to a group of saurischians called the theropods. Most theropods walked on two legs and had larger brains than other dinosaurs (relative to their body size). Scientists think that these things helped them become great hunters. Some theropods, such as *Confuciusornis* [con-FYOO-shus-OR-nis], were tiny; others, like *Tyrannosaurus*, were gigantic. We can see so much of God's imagination and creativity in this group!

Genus: ALLOSAURUS
[AL-uh-SORE-us]
Lived: late Jurassic period
Length: up to 39 feet
Weight: up to 2.2 tons

> You [God] are great and powerful, glorious, splendid, and majestic. Everything in heaven and earth is yours, and you are king, supreme ruler over all.
> 1 Chronicles 29:11 TLB

ALLOSAURUS

Remember Big Al on p. 16? *Allosaurus*'s fossilized bones were some of the first to be found showing hollow spaces within them, like modern birds' bones. This impressive hunter had teeth as sharp as steak knives. If one tooth fell out while fighting, no problem: *Allosaurus* could regrow teeth!

FUN FACT

Special 3D X-rays of fossils have shown that many dinosaurs had replacement teeth standing by inside their jawbones, like modern-day sharks.

BIG TEETH, BIG ATTITUDE?

TYRANNOSAURUS REX

Tyrannosaurus rex was one of the largest meat-eaters ever to roam the Earth. Some stood as tall as a giraffe. This dinosaur had an incredibly strong bite and teeth up to 11 inches long!

FAST MOVERS

Tyrannosaurus rex was huge and heavy but also pretty fast. It's tricky to say exactly *how* fast because we can't watch it move. Its bone structure and footprints mean some scientists think that T. rex could run as fast as 27 miles per hour! Others think that it couldn't run at all, but could still walk as fast as most humans can run because of its long legs.

DINO BATTLE?

Tyrannosaurus and *Allosaurus* were two of God's top predators. They never met because *Allosaurus* lived around 80 million years before T. rex came along. But, if they *had* met and fought, the larger, heavier T. rex would probably have beaten *Allosaurus* hands down!

Genus: TYRANNOSAURUS
[tie-RAN-oh-SORE-us]
Lived: late Cretaceous period
Length: up to 42.6 feet
Weight: up to 10.5 tons

SQUISHY SECRETS

Sometimes science leads us to seriously surprising discoveries about God's amazing world. In the 1990s, Dr. Mary Schweitzer, a Christian and professor of paleontology in the USA, found something incredible.

While looking at T. rex fossil bones under a **microscope**, she found what looked like fossilized blood cells. While this dinosaur was alive, its blood cells would have been soft, like its skin, muscles, and other squishy parts. Usually, we only find fossils of the hard parts of God's ancient creatures, so Dr. Schweitzer's discovery was very surprising!

Her findings changed what we know about how things fossilize and showed that we might be able to learn more about dinosaurs than we ever thought possible! This kind of exciting discovery could help us answer big questions about what dinosaurs were like and how they interacted with their ancient environments.

Dr. Schweitzer loves to use her science to find out more about the marvelous dinosaurs God has made. She says, "I do science to honor God by discovering the truth about how he created. The more I understand how things work, the bigger God gets."

SINK OR SWIM?

SPINOSAURUS

One of the wonderfully exciting things about hunting for fossils in God's great creation is that you never know what you're going to find next!

Genus: SPINOSAURUS
[SPY-no-SORE-us]
Lived: Cretaceous period
Length: up to 52.5 feet
Weight: up to 13 tons

In 1912, paleontologists in Egypt unearthed a fossil unlike anything anyone had seen before. The dinosaur was a meat-eating theropod, but it seemed to have unusually powerful arms, a huge sail on its back, and a head like a crocodile. Was it a swimmer? What was the sail for? What could we learn about this marvelous creature?

Sadly, this Egyptian fossil was destroyed in the Second World War. Since then, more *Spinosaurus* fossils have been found and studied, but the mysteries are far from solved.

There's still a lot to discover about this amazing part of God's imaginative creation. In or out of the water, *Spinosaurus* must have been a wondrous sight!

A STRONG SWIMMER?

Spinosaurus seems to have had webbed feet, a strong, flexible tail, and a mouth full of cone-shaped teeth. These features would have been great for swimming and catching fish. What about that remarkable sail? Some scientists suggest it would have helped *Spinosaurus* to swim and hunt in the water. But was it really a swimming dinosaur?

BOBBING AND DIVING

Computer models of *Spinosaurus* show that it could probably float with its head above water, perhaps bobbing around like a cork. But scientists aren't sure how well it could dive or swim underwater. Some think its powerful tail would have helped it swim through the water like an alligator. Others think it wouldn't even have been able to stay upright in the water, let alone swim.

SHORELINE STROLLER

We don't yet have enough evidence to know exactly how *Spinosaurus* lived. At the moment, scientists think that *Spinosaurus* was well suited to living and hunting along shorelines of lakes, seas, or rivers, either in or out of the water. But it probably didn't live in the water all the time.

DUCK-BILLED DINOSAURS

If it looked like a duck (and quite possibly sounded like a duck), it just might have been . . . a hadrosaur!

Hadrosaurs, or duck-billed dinosaurs, were a big group of ornithischian dinosaurs with wide, duck-like beaks and special rows of teeth shaped a bit like giant nail files to grind up tough veggies. Fossils show that they usually walked on all four feet, holding their tails up behind them, but that sometimes they stood upright on their back legs.

There were lots of similarities between hadrosaurs, but they didn't all look the same. Different hadrosaurs had very different styles of crests on their heads. Just look at *Brachylophosaurus*, *Parasaurolophus*, and *Lambeosaurus* (see p. 19).

HADROSAUR MYSTERY

Hadrosaurs have presented a particular mystery over the years. Their fossils show many, many different types of crests, and so at first, paleontologists thought each type of crest represented a different type of hadrosaur. But in 1975, Dr. Peter Dodson, who had studied lots of these fossils, suggested that there probably weren't so many different types. Like the *Pachycephalosaurus* (see p. 27), it seems that some hadrosaurs had differently shaped crests depending on how old they were and whether they were male or female.

New fossils are being found all the time, helping scientists form a clearer picture of the dinosaur family and the wonders and details of God's creation.

Parasauralophus

THE STORY OF LEONARDO

In 2000, during the last hour of a summer dig in Montana, amateur dinosaur hunter Dan Stephenson found a bone sticking out of a sandy bank. Dan called Nate Murphy, a paleontology curator at a nearby museum, to help him work out what he had found. It was only later that they came to realize just how special it was!

Leonardo (named after some nearby graffiti) was a three- or four-year-old *Brachylophosaurus*, one of the duck-billed hadrosaurs. Because of the conditions where he died, Leonardo dried out before he was fossilized, creating an especially well-preserved fossil, like a giant dinosaur

mummy! When he was discovered, Leonardo had thick, stony skin covering his fossilized insides. This amazing fossil answers many more questions than normal dinosaur fossils do. Scientists have used special **X-rays** to see inside Leonardo's stomach, heart, and guts. They even learned what he had been snacking on—ferns and conifers.

Extra-special fossils like this are rare. When Leonardo was found, he was one of only four "dino-mummies" ever to have been discovered.

PRAYER
Thank you, God, for the wonderful processes of your world that have let us learn so much about Leonardo the *Brachylophosaurus*.

Brachylophosaurus

DUCK-BILLED DINOSAURS

AN "EGGS"-TRAORDINARY DISCOVERY

In 1978, Marion Brandvold and her family were hunting for fossils on a ranch in Montana when they discovered something spectacular: the first baby dinosaur bones ever found in North America.

Paleontologist Jack Horner visited the rock shop owned by Marion and her family and spotted the bones stored in an old coffee tin. He asked where they had come from. Marion showed the site to him and his team and they began to explore.

A volunteer named Fran Tannenbaum found the first fossilized dinosaur eggs in the Western hemisphere on the site, which is now called Egg Mountain. Dr. Horner's team was also the first in the world to discover dinosaur nests. Egg Mountain had been a nesting ground for over ten thousand duck-billed hadrosaurs, called *Maiasaura*.

HORNER IN HOLLYWOOD

The character of paleontologist Alan Grant in the film *Jurassic Park* was modeled on Jack Horner. Dr. Horner was also a consultant to Steven Spielberg for the film.

MAIASAURA

Maiasaura, a hadrosaur with a flat beak and a wide nose, was first discovered on Egg Mountain. Areas like this—with extra-special fossils—can show us much more than simply what God's dinosaurs looked like. They can also tell us things about how some dinosaurs behaved and what they were like as babies. We now know that groups of *Maiasaura* lived and built their nests together, like colonies of giant penguins. They seem to have nested on high ground to protect their babies from carnivores. The babies may have been just one foot long when they hatched, and their parents probably looked after them until they got bigger—just like lots of their bird relatives living today.

Genus: MAIASAURA
[MY-uh-SORE-uh]
Lived: late Cretaceous period
Length: up to 29.5 feet
Weight: up to 4.4 tons

RACING RAPTORS

OVIRAPTOR

The first *Oviraptor* fossil was discovered in 1923 by paleontologist Roy Chapman Andrews in Mongolia. Its name means "egg hunter," and the name was chosen because the fossil was found on a pile of what looked like *Protoceratops* eggs. Some paleontologists weren't sure *Oviraptor* was really an egg thief, so they kept asking questions. In the 1990s, scientists discovered fossils of some *Oviraptor* relatives sitting on nests like birds. This suggested that the original eggs actually belonged to *Oviraptor*! It seems these theropods were guarding their *own* eggs, not stealing someone else's.

FUN FACT
Oviraptor's long legs probably helped it run fast, a bit like an ostrich, which can run over 30 miles per hour!

Genus: OVIRAPTOR
[OH-vuh-RAP-tore]
Lived: late Cretaceous period
Length: up to 6.5 feet
Weight: up to 128 pounds

ROY CHAPMAN ANDREWS

Roy Chapman Andrews discovered other dinosaurs too, including the first known *Velociraptor*. In 1922, he led a dangerous expedition to the Gobi Desert, at the edge of Mongolia. After getting lost, his team stumbled across some incredible cliffs filled with dinosaur fossils. There, they found the first ancient dinosaur eggs ever seen!

VELOCIRAPTOR

Small and covered in feathers, *Velociraptor* was part of a theropod family called the Dromaeosauridae [DROH-me-oh-SORE-ih-day]. Scientists think many small carnivorous dinosaurs, like *Velociraptor*, were intelligent and hunted in groups—like today's wolves. With quick brains, sharp teeth, and top speeds of around 25 miles per hour, packs of these raptors would have been impressive hunters.

Genus: VELOCIRAPTOR
[veh-LAH-suh-RAP-tore]
Lived: late Cretaceous period
Length: up to 9.8 feet
Weight: up to 99 pounds

ROBERT BAKKER

Christian paleontologist Dr. Robert Bakker loves discovering more about dinosaurs, especially raptors. He says, "Bones and rocks are eloquent storytellers, if you know how to listen to them."

WHY DID GOD CREATE CARNIVORES?

We don't always like the idea of animals eating each other, but what does God think? The Bible doesn't tell us why there are carnivores, but it does say God provides food for them and loves all his creatures.

Carnivores are actually really important. When an animal is eaten, whether by huge dinosaurs or tiny flies, the **nutrients** in its body end up in the soil, supporting new plant and animal lives.

A BETTER FUTURE?

It's still hard to understand why God might have made the world this way. The Bible does say that things aren't perfect yet—its writers talk about all of creation waiting for a better future. It also says that, because **Jesus** died and came back to life again, creation will one day be made new and better than we could imagine, with no more pain, death, or suffering. Maybe this means that things will be different for carnivores.

We know God loves the whole of creation, so we can trust that this promise will be wonderful for all creation, including his carnivores.

> But we are looking forward to God's promise of new heavens and a new earth afterwards, where there will be only goodness.
> 2 Peter 3:13 TLB

FEATHERS AND FLYING

ARCHAEOPTERYX

Like some of God's other meat-eating theropods, *Archaeopteryx* had sharp teeth and clawed fingers and toes. It wasn't big, like T. rex, or a fearsome pack hunter, like *Velociraptor*, but *Archaeopteryx* was one of the first examples of feathery dinosaurs ever found. Fossils show that it had a long, feathered tail, feathery back legs, and wings for flying or gliding. It wouldn't have been as good at flying as many modern birds, but scientists do think that it could fly for short periods.

Genus: ARCHAEOPTERYX
[ARK-ee-OP-tuh-rix]
Lived: late Jurassic period
Length: up to 1.6 feet
Weight: up to 2.2 pounds

Genus: SINOSAUROPTERYX
[SIGH-no-sore-OP-tuh-rix]
Lived: early Cretaceous period
Length: up to 3.6 feet
Weight: up to 2.2 pounds

SINOSAUROPTERYX

In the 1990s, a farmer in China found a fossil of the earliest feathered dinosaur ever discovered, *Sinosauropteryx*. This little theropod had unusually short arms and a very long tail. Its feathers were very simple and wouldn't have helped it to fly or glide. But its fossil was so well preserved that scientists could tell its long tail was stripy—with light and dark bands of color that might have helped it to stay camouflaged.

AMAZING PRESERVATION, ASTOUNDING DISCOVERIES!

The discovery of *Sinosauropteryx* brought many paleontologists to China's Liaoning Province to search for similar fossils. What they found was extraordinary! Ash and mud from millions of years of volcanic eruptions had preserved many of God's plants and animals, including the parts that normally rot away, like feathers. Many of the feathered dinosaurs we know about were found in Liaoning. Scientists now think it's likely that many, maybe all, of God's theropod dinosaurs had some sort of feathers.

YUTYRANNUS

Yutyrannus is one of the largest feathery dinosaurs found so far and, like many others, it couldn't fly. Its arms weren't built like wings—they were far too small. So why were the little evolutionary changes that gave these flightless theropods feathers so useful? Maybe their feathers helped them to stay warm or show off, like colorful birds do today . . . or both. We need more evidence to know for sure.

Genus: YUTYRANNUS
[YOO-ty-RAN-us]
Lived: early Cretaceous period
Length: up to 29.5 feet
Weight: 1.5 tons

PRAYER

Thank you, God, for your wonderful creation. Thank you for the way fossils form and help us learn more about your creatures that lived millions of years ago!

CAIHONG

This duck-sized theropod had a long, narrow head with a bony crest. Ribbon-like feathers covered its body and it had long tail feathers. But that's not the most amazing thing about this dinosaur. Incredibly well-preserved fossils and clever science have shown that its feathers shimmered and sparkled in the light, like hummingbird feathers. It's no surprise, then, that *Caihong* is Mandarin for "rainbow."

Genus: CAIHONG
[KY-hong]
Lived: late Jurassic period
Length: up to 1.3 feet
Weight: up to one pound

God has made such beautiful creatures. What are some of your favorites?

43

The plant-eating sauropods are the very biggest of God's dinosaurs that we have found, and were probably the biggest creatures ever to walk the Earth. Some of today's whales are heavier (more than 110 tons) but sauropods include the longest animals ever discovered.

The giant sauropods were all saurischians. Fossils found together show us that some of them—including *Apatosaurus*, *Camarasaurus*, and *Diplodocus*—lived together in North America in the late Jurassic period. Maybe they grazed happily together in herds. What an incredible sight that would have been!

APATOSAURUS

Apatosaurus means "deceptive lizard." It was given this name because some of its bones are a bit like those of the mosasaurs [MOH-zuh-sores], which were big, ancient sea reptiles (see p. 50).

GENTLE GIANT

Apatosaurus was huge! It traveled in herds, browsing the highest forest leaves, and was too large to be in danger of attack from anything around at the time, even an adult *Allosaurus*.

Genus: APATOSAURUS
[ah-PAH-tuh-SORE-us]
Lived: late Jurassic period
Length: up to 75.5 feet
Weight: up to 38.5 tons

44

CAMARASAURUS

Camarasaurus means "chambered lizard," named because of the big openings in its vertebrae (back bones). These openings, which we see in lots of other dinosaurs too, were probably for "air sacs" connected to their lungs. Many modern birds have these to help them get lots of oxygen into their bodies. The openings also make their bones lighter. That would have been especially useful for these giant dinosaurs.

Genus: CAMARASAURUS
[KAM-a-ra-SORE-us]
Lived: late Jurassic period
Length: up to 65.6 feet
Weight: up to 16.5 tons

THE LARGEST LAND ANIMALS

Today's largest land animals are African elephants, but the biggest they get is only about 23 feet long, weighing around 6.6 tons. That's not half as big as some of these giant dinosaurs!

Diplodocus

These spectacular sauropods were really big and powerful. But can you imagine how much bigger God, who created them all, must be?

Do you not know? Have you not heard? The LORD is an eternal God, the creator of the whole earth. He does not get tired or weary; there is no limit to his wisdom.
Isaiah 40:28 NET

DIPLODOCUS

Diplodocus is one of the most famous of God's sauropods. For many years, it was the longest dinosaur to have been discovered (turn the page for some even bigger discoveries). Some scientists think that it might have used its tail like a whip to fight off predators such as *Allosaurus*.

Genus: DIPLODOCUS
[di-PLOD-oh-kus]
Lived: late Jurassic period
Length: up to 85 feet
Weight: up to 22 tons

SUPERSIZED SAUROPODS

LEDUMAHADI

In 2018, paleontologists announced that they'd found a new dinosaur in South Africa. They named it *Ledumahadi*, which means "a giant thunderclap" in Sesotho, one of the South African languages. *Ledumahadi* wasn't a sauropod, but it was a close relative. This saurischian is the largest land animal we have discovered from the early Jurassic period, about twice the size of today's biggest elephants. *Ledumahadi* is particularly interesting because its legs are different from those of its sauropod cousins. This means that we can study the different ways legs developed to support huge, heavy dinosaurs.

PATAGOTITAN

In 2017, paleontologists officially named a massive sauropod that might be one of the biggest ever discovered. It's unusual to find whole fossilized skeletons of animals that large, as parts often get lost over time. But the remains of *Patagotitan* (found in Patagonia, Argentina) were surprisingly complete, helping scientists get to know these enormous beasts.

◄ **Genus: PATAGOTITAN**
[PAT-uh-go-TY-tun]
Lived: late Cretaceous period
Length: up to 102 feet
Weight: up to 80 tons

> O Lord God! You have made the heavens and earth by your great power; nothing is too hard for you!
> Jeremiah 32:17 TLB

◄ **Genus: LEDUMAHADI**
[Leh-DOO-mah-HAD-ee]
Lived: early Jurassic period
Length: unknown
Weight: up to 13 tons

HOW DID THESE DINOSAURS GET SO BIG?

God's special processes of evolution mean each new creature is a little bit different from its parents. Over time, these little differences add up to some big ones. In the case of the magnificent sauropods, one big difference is just how *big* they were! But what were the little changes that gradually helped them get so big?

LONG NECKS

Even some of the smaller, early sauropods had quite long necks. This may have let them reach food that others couldn't. We can also tell that they could swallow lots of food without chewing. Those two things might have helped sauropods get enough food to nourish larger bodies.

FUN FACT

Sauropods were really tall, but it's hard to tell from the fossils just how bendy their long necks were or how high they could reach. Scientists still don't know for sure.

BIGGER AND BIGGER

Like us, many animals do most of their growing in a relatively short period of time, then stay around the same size. But some dinosaurs kept growing for much longer. Some of these giant sauropods might have kept growing for 30 to 40 years.

◀ Leg bone from a *Patagotitan*

DEEP BREATH

Scientists also think that many ancient dinosaurs had a special breathing system (see *Camarasaurus*, p. 45) that helped them take in lots of oxygen. For smaller dinosaurs, this probably helped them to move quickly, but a good air supply could also have helped the huge body get enough oxygen.

This and other differences seem to have worked together to allow God's sauropods to reach larger and larger sizes. And because being bigger helped to keep them safe from most carnivores, it became more and more common within the sauropod group.

God's imaginative creation has been filled with such magnificent creatures. Isn't it wonderful how we can learn about them through his gift of science? Keep reading to find out more about some of the animals that lived alongside the dinosaurs.

God didn't only make the dinosaurs. Just as there are lots of different kinds of creatures living alongside today's dinosaurs (birds, see p. 21), they definitely weren't alone during the Mesozoic era.

DINOSAUR COMPANIONS

Most dinosaurs spent their time on land alongside other land animals, including scuttling insects, slinking lizards, and even fluffy early mammals. The lakes, rivers, and oceans were filled with life too, like aquatic insects, shellfish, and other **invertebrates** [in-VER-tih-brayts] (animals without backbones).

There were also incredible predators with amazing names, such as *Koolasuchus* [cool-uh-SOOK-us], *Gobiops* [GO-bee-ops], and *Xenobrachyops* [ZEN-oh-BRACK-ee-ops]. These ancient creatures were the ancestors of today's amphibians (like frogs and salamanders). They lived much like crocodiles do and would have been fierce hunters in the shallow waters.

Koolasuchus

PRAYER

God has filled the world with such incredible animals. Do you have a favorite ancient creature? Why not take a moment to thank God for some of the wonderful living things he has made.

SOMETHING FISHY

There were plenty of fish swimming around in God's Mesozoic oceans. They can be just as mysterious and tricky to find out about as the dinosaurs!

Leedsichthys [leed-SICK-thiss], a giant Jurassic swimmer, was first found fossilized in Peterborough, England. Only fragments of skeletons have been found, but it may have been up to 52.5 feet long.

HIDING IN THE DEPTHS

Another mysterious fish is the coelacanth [SEE-luh-kanth]. In the 1830s, paleontologists began to discover fossils of a roughly 6.5 foot-long fish that we now know first lived more than 400 million years ago. Like most ancient creatures, it seemed coelacanths had been extinct for millions of years. But in 1939, museum curator Marjorie Courtenay-Latimer discovered that an African fisherman had caught a live coelacanth. Paleontologists were amazed. After all these years, coelacanths were not extinct. Some types are alive even today!

PREHISTORIC SEAS

MARINE REPTILES

A whole variety of God's Mesozoic animals were marine reptiles, including groups you might have heard of, such as ichthyosaurs, mosasaurs, and plesiosaurs [PLEASE-ee-oh-sores]. They were reptiles, but they weren't dinosaurs. Just like whales and dolphins are descended from land-based mammals, the ancestors of these marine reptiles had lived on land before lots of little changes over many generations made them well adapted for life in the sea.

Mosasaurus

MOSASAURS

Mosasaurs were fearsome predators of the late Cretaceous oceans. At up to 56 feet long, these sea monsters ate sharks, turtles, fish, squid, and just about anything they wanted—even smaller mosasaurs! Like other marine reptiles, such as sea turtles and alligators, mosasaurs had to breathe air from the surface but they probably didn't come onto land at all.

Praise the LORD from the earth, you great sea creatures and all ocean depths.
Psalm 148:7 NIV

WATER BIRTH

It's very exciting when fossils show us more about God's ancient animals than just what they looked like. Paleontologists have discovered that at least some mosasaurs and ichthyosaurs gave birth to live young rather than laying eggs. They even think some plesiosaurs might have looked after their young.

MARY ANNING: FOSSIL HUNTER

Mary Anning grew up on the Dorset coast (an excellent place for fossil hunting in England) in the early 1800s. As a child, she started looking for fossils (then called "curiosities") to sell to tourists, but soon became an expert fossil hunter! She found some of the first toothy ichthyosaurs, winged pterosaurs [TERR-uh-sores], and the very first full fossil of a long-necked plesiosaur.

FAMILY AND FAITH

Mary's family was too poor for her to spend much time at school, but she was a Christian and learned to read and write at church. Back then, women weren't allowed to study at college, but she read scientific papers and taught herself about ancient creatures and the fossils they left behind.

Mary's faith was important to her. She spent lots of time thinking about God and reading the Bible, as well as exploring the world she believed God made.

NEW DISCOVERIES, NEW IDEAS

Her discoveries helped scientists understand how things have changed over time and see that different creatures had lived in God's creation at different times. That was still quite a new idea in those days.

REMEMBERING MARY

Mary's work changed science forever and some of her fossils can still be seen in museums today. At the time, men often took credit for her discoveries, leaving her out of their scientific papers. But after she died, a stained-glass window with images of Mary and her fossils was put up in the local church to remember who she was and the way she added to our scientific understanding of God's world.

FUN FACT

In 2010, a major science academy called the Royal Society listed Mary as one of the top ten British women who helped to shape modern science. Many women have made important contributions to science, so this is quite an achievement.

PREHISTORIC SEAS

ICHTHYOSAURS

Ichthyosaurs were a group of dolphin-like marine reptiles. Many different types lived between the early Triassic and the late Cretaceous periods. Early ichthyosaurs were about as long as an adult man is tall, but some later types grew much bigger. *Shonisaurus* [SHOW-ni-SORE-us], for example, grew up to 69 feet long—that's as long as a submarine!

> How many are your works, Lord! In wisdom you made them all; the earth is full of your creatures. There is the sea, vast and spacious, teeming with creatures beyond number!
> Psalm 104:24–25 NIV

Shonisaurus

SHARP-EYED SWIMMERS

Millions of years have passed since ichthyosaurs swam God's oceans, but fossils give amazing insights into how they lived. We think that they might have been good at hunting at night, or perhaps in the dark ocean depths, because many ichthyosaur fossils show that they had massive eyes, protected by special bony rings. Their eyes were larger than soccer balls—bigger than those of any other known **vertebrate**!

WHEN IS A DOLPHIN NOT A DOLPHIN?

Ichthyosaurs and dolphins may *look* similar, but they are nowhere near each other on the family tree of animal life. Ichthyosaurs are reptiles and dolphins are mammals. The little changes that happen in God's evolutionary processes mean we sometimes find that animals living in similar environments look similar, even if they're not closely related. We call this **convergent evolution**. With dolphins and ichthyosaurs, little changes led to both groups developing a streamlined shape, long noses, pointed teeth, flipper-like "arms," reduced back legs, and many other similar features.

PLESIOSAURS

Elasmosaurus is one of the best-known plesiosaurs. This late Cretaceous creature had a long tail but a *really* long neck, about 23 feet long. It is one of the longest-necked animals ever found, with 72 neck vertebrae (bones)—humans have just 7 of these!

Elasmosaurus was discovered by Edward Drinker Cope (see p. 23 for more of his "bone wars" rivalry with Othniel Charles March). The first pictures he drew and published showed its head at the wrong end! He later redrew the pictures after scientists studied the fossils further and realized the mistake.

Genus: ELASMOSAURUS
[eh-LAZ-moh-SORE-us]
Lived: late Cretaceous period
Length: up to 42.6 feet
Weight: up to 15 tons

BIG HEAD OR LONG NECK?

Plesiosaurs came in two main forms. The pliosauromorph [PLY-oh-SORE-oh-morf], such as the brilliantly named *Pliosaurus funkei* (also known as "Predator X"), had a big head, short neck, and powerful flippers.

Genus: PLIOSAURUS
(Species: funkei)
[PLY-oh-sore-us FUNK-ey]
Lived: late Jurassic period
Length: up to 42.6 feet
Weight: unknown

The plesiosauromorph [PLEASE-ee-oh-SORE-oh-morf], like *Elasmosaurus*, had a small head and much longer neck. Many of the varieties of this form had large front flippers to pull themselves through the water, but compared to the pliosauromorphs, they were quite slow and only hunted small sea animals.

PREHISTORIC SKIES

God's Mesozoic skies were teeming with life! Insects flitted about and, alongside some flying dinosaurs (including early birds), other reptiles soared. These marvelous flying reptiles, called pterosaurs, were a completely different group from the dinosaurs, showing us even more of God's creativity and imagination.

Genus: PTERODACTYLUS
[TERR-uh-DACK-till-us]
Lived: late Jurassic period
Wingspan: up to 5 feet
Weight: up to 1.8 pounds

PTERODACTYLUS

Pterodactylus (often called pterodactyl [TERR-uh-DACK-till]) was the first pterosaur to be discovered. It was quite small for a pterosaur, with a long beak full of little, sharp teeth that probably helped it hunt fish and other small creatures. Like other pterosaurs, its wings were more like bat wings than bird wings, with stretched skin and muscle joining a special long finger to its back leg.

DISTINCTIVE DIFFERENCES

Some pterosaurs were as small as blue jays, others were giants of the sky. They had all kinds of differently shaped crests on their heads, and ate different things too. Some ate insects, fruit, or land animals. Some had beaks with needle-like teeth for catching fish. Others had filters (like some whales do) to sift tiny bugs and shrimp from the water. Some pterosaurs may even have been able to swim a little, as well as fly.

Everything belongs to the LORD your God, not only the earth and everything on it, but also the sky and the highest heavens.
Deuteronomy 10:14 CEV

FURRY FLYERS

Many pterosaur fossils show a covering of fuzzy fibers different from mammal hair or bird feathers, called "pycnofibers" [PICK-no-fy-bers]. Scientists think pycnofibers probably helped to keep pterosaurs warm.

QUETZALCOATLUS

Quetzalcoatlus is one of the largest of God's flying creatures yet discovered. Its huge wings helped it glide, like a massive eagle. Some studies suggest *Quetzalcoatlus* could fly faster than a speedy cheetah and could fly for a week without resting!

Genus: QUETZALCOATLUS
[KHET-zul-ko-AT-lus]
Lived: late Cretaceous period
Wingspan: up to 36 feet
Weight: up to a half ton

Genus: RHAMPHORHYNCHUS
[RAM-fo-RINK-us]
Lived: late Jurassic period
Wingspan: up to 6.5 feet
Weight: up to 10.6 ounces

RHAMPHORHYNCHUS

Rhamphorhynchus and its relatives didn't just have wings—their back legs were also joined together by a flap of skin and muscle to help them fly. This could have made walking awkward, but their strong claws suggest that they might have spent more time climbing in the trees than walking on the ground.

NEMICOLOPTERUS

The only *Nemicolopterus* fossil found so far is very small. Scientists think that it was almost fully grown, so *Nemicolopterus* might be one of the smallest pterosaurs we've found.

Genus: NEMICOLOPTERUS
[NEM-ee-co-LOP-tuh-rus]
Lived: early Cretaceous period
Wingspan: up to 9.8 inches
Weight: unknown

PTEROSAUR NESTS

We call baby pterosaurs "flaplings" and they are fascinating. Pterosaurs seem to have laid delicate, soft-shelled eggs. These didn't fossilize well, so there aren't many to study. Scientists think that some nested in large colonies and many probably buried their eggs, like lots of modern reptiles. Flaplings may have been flightless at first, needing adult care. But some evidence suggests that they could possibly walk, fly, and look after themselves soon after hatching—there's a lot still to learn!

God's Mesozoic world was filled with incredible animals, but even before the dinosaurs, God was using his clever evolutionary processes to fill the earth with many different creatures.

EARLY EUPELYCOSAURS

Before the Mesozoic era of the dinosaurs, in the Permian [PER-me-un] period, early eupelycosaurs [YOU-PELL-ee-ko-sores], such as *Dimetrodon* [die-MET-ro-don], ruled the earth.

Compared to lots of the dinosaurs, *Dimetrodon* and its relatives were slow movers. Their legs splayed out like those of lizards, unlike dinosaurs, who stood taller and held their legs closer to their bodies, like today's mammals do, which is better for running and turning.

Dimetrodon

WHO-PELYCOSAUR?

Eupelycosaurs were probably cold-blooded—like snakes, turtles, crocodiles, and other modern reptiles—needing to sit in the sun to become warm and active.

But these early eupelycosaurs weren't actually closely related to today's reptiles or even the dinosaurs. These creatures that lived long before the dinosaurs were, in fact, ancestors of today's mammals! Isn't it astonishing to learn about our history reaching way, way back in God's creation?

THERAPSIDS

One interesting group of eupelycosaurs were the therapsids [thur-AP-sids], which seem to have first appeared at least 20 million years before God's dinosaurs. By studying how these fascinating animals evolved over time, we see some little changes that have shaped modern mammals. Generation by generation, the legs of some types of therapsid were held more closely to their bodies than before and they gradually began to become more like warm-blooded animals. Their teeth were arranged similarly to today's dogs or lions, and some of them also had fur. Early therapsids also came in many shapes and sizes.

ANTEOSAURUS

One of the largest we've found was *Anteosaurus* [ANT-ee-oh-SORE-us], which grew to over 16 feet long.

CISTECEPHALUS

Cistecephalus [SIS-tuh-SEF-uh-lus] was much smaller, less than 2 feet long, and used its strong front legs for digging burrows.

CYNODONTS

The cynodonts [SY-no-donts] were a dog-like group of God's therapsids, and fossils have been found in Africa, Asia, Europe, North America, South America, and even Antarctica. Many of these marvelous creatures lived alongside the dinosaurs. Some might look a little familiar.

OLIGOKYPHUS

Oligokyphus [OLL-ee-go-KY-fuss] was a herbivorous weasel-like cynodont.

THRINAXODON

Fox-sized *Thrinaxodon* [thry-NAX-oh-don] was a carnivore that probably ate insects and small herbivores and may have been furry.

CYNOGNATHUS

Cynognathus [SY-nog-NATH-us], and some other cynodonts, may even have had whiskers!

PRAYER
All-powerful God, thank you that every moment of your creation, and every single creature, is awesome, wonderful, and precious to you.

We now know that all mammals, from elephants to mice (and even humans!), are part of this group. Through God's creative processes, lots of little changes over many generations have led to exciting diversity among the cynodonts. How incredible to be part of such a fantastically diverse family!

All kinds of amazing dinosaurs roamed God's Mesozoic world, but only birds are still around. Where did the others go?

Most became extinct (completely died out) about 66 million years ago, along with many other living things.

EXTINCTION: ENDINGS AND BEGINNINGS

God's clever evolutionary processes mean every moment on Earth has a unique combination of living things. Little evolutionary changes add up over time, meaning many creatures are so different from their ancestors that we think of them as completely new species. When no members of a species are around anymore, we say that it has become extinct.

Sometimes a species becomes extinct because the **environment** changes too quickly or too many of them are killed, so not enough babies are born to keep the species going. This can be sad. But the Earth's history has been full of new species emerging, so the wonderfully diverse mixture of life on Earth has continued to grow and change.

[God] You are kind and patient and always loving. You are good to everyone, and you take care of all your creation.
Psalm 145:8–9 CEV

HUMAN RESPONSIBILITY

Humans weren't around when most dinosaurs became extinct, but we have a huge impact on God's world today. Sadly, the way humans have treated God's creation has caused many species to become extinct and has made it harder for new ones to thrive. God asks humans to look after his creation, so it's important that we play our part well.

MASS EXTINCTION EVENTS

Over time, thousands of dinosaur species have existed. Many became extinct in the "usual" ways—but sometimes unusual events cause many species to die out around the same time. We call these "mass extinction events."

About 66 million years ago, at the end of the Cretaceous period, one of these events wiped out around 75 percent of life on Earth, including all the non-bird dinosaurs.

THRIVING SURVIVORS

Species that survive mass extinctions can evolve and spread out quickly, as there is less competition than normal. In fact, without a mass extinction at the end of the Triassic period, dinosaurs may never have become so diverse or ruled God's Jurassic and Cretaceous periods.

WHY WOULD GOD LET THE DINOSAURS DIE?

The Bible says that God loves everything he creates, so it can be hard to understand why he would let things end or die.

CYCLES OF LIFE

God delights in everything that he has made, including his dinosaurs, which have roamed the Earth for more than 240 million years. He is a patient creator, using processes that unfold over billions of years involving lots of change. And his whole universe is based on cycles of life and death that support future life.

If stars didn't come to an end, exploding into space after burning for millions of years, there would be none of the "stardust" that makes up planets, new stars, and even life on Earth! And if living things didn't die and pass nutrients back into the soil, new plants and animals wouldn't be able to live.

The extinction of non-bird dinosaurs made space for groups of tiny, mammal-like creatures to develop and fill the world with thousands of new mammal species. So without the extinction of most of the dinosaurs, there might never have been whales, pangolins, or even humans.

BIG QUESTIONS

We don't really know why God's universe works this way. But, as we think about it, it's important to remember that God is good. He really cares and understands sadness and pain. And he promises that, one day, things will be different (see p. 41). So we can trust him, even as we explore big, difficult—and sometimes painful—questions.

CLIMATE CHANGE CLUES

Each mass extinction event seems to have involved big or quick changes in the climate. If it gets too hot or cold, lots of plants die, and herbivores struggle to find enough food. And if they die, then carnivores also go hungry.

Climate change can happen for many reasons. The surface of God's Earth is made of huge, curved slabs of rocks called tectonic [tek-TAH-nik] plates. These slowly moving plates form oceans, mountains, and islands, as well as change weather patterns, and cause earthquakes and volcanic eruptions—all things that can change the climate, sometimes very quickly.

Living things can also have an impact on the climate. When plants started to evolve and spread on land, they changed the **atmosphere** by sucking in carbon dioxide and releasing oxygen. This led to "global cooling," significantly changing life on Earth. Those early plants were fossilized—not into rocks but into coal, oil, and gas, which is why we call them "fossil fuels." Today, humans use these fuels. This releases carbon dioxide back into the atmosphere, causing "global warming," once again creating a serious impact on life on earth.

Scientists think that the mass extinction of the non-bird dinosaurs involved both volcanic activity and atmospheric change, but believe something else also played a role . . .

EXAMINING THE EXTRATERRESTRIAL

There's a lot out there in God's enormous universe. Usually only little bits of space dust make it through Earth's protective atmosphere, but sometimes much larger space rocks have a bigger impact.

About 66 million years ago, at the end of the Cretaceous period, a giant asteroid (or maybe a comet) at least six miles wide slammed into Mexico's Yucatan Peninsula. The crash caused giant ocean waves, started wildfires, and flung huge amounts of dust, rocks, and gas into the atmosphere. It also caused massive earthquakes and volcanic eruptions, releasing even more gas, dust, and ash, blocking out the sun and causing extreme global cooling.

The impact might have killed some things instantly. But many species probably died out gradually because of the global climate change it caused.

PRAYER

Dear God, please help me remember that you are good and you love everything you have created, including me. Help me trust your plans, even when I'm sad or confused about the way things end. Thank you for the amazing variety of living things you have made and the processes that have shaped them. Thank you too for the gift of science, so we can enjoy finding out about your wonderful creatures.

INVESTIGATING IRIDIUM

Iridium [ih-RID-ee-um] is a silvery-white metal that is very rare in Earth rocks, but much more common in space rocks. There's a lot of it in a thin rock layer that was laid down all around the world about 66 million years ago. Scientists think that this layer formed when dust from a big space rock impact was flung into the atmosphere, spreading out and settling down all over the Earth.

Below the iridium layer there are lots of dinosaur fossils, but we don't find any non-bird dinosaurs in the newer rock layers above it. This suggests that the space rock impact played a major role in the extinction of the non-bird dinosaurs.

WHAT HAPPENED NEXT?

Not all living things died out 66 million years ago. As well as some early mammals, and the group of dinosaurs we call birds, survivors included crocodiles, frogs, snakes, lizards, turtles, insects, fish, lots of plants, and bacteria. Scientists think that many little things probably worked together to protect them—including where they lived, what they ate, and how easily they could keep warm and hide from predators! God's creative evolutionary processes mean that these surviving groups evolved over generations to fill the Earth with all kinds of fascinating new animals, each one made and loved by God.

God's wondrous world has so many incredible mysteries to uncover. The more we learn through science, the more we realize that there is still more to explore!

How wonderful are the things the LORD does! All who are delighted with them want to understand them.
Psalm 111:2 TLB

Geiger counter

NEW GADGETS

In the past, paleontologists had to rely on hammers, chisels, and shovels to study God's dinosaurs. But now we have brilliant new gadgets to help too.

Sensors called Geiger counters can use **radiation** patterns to detect some fossils while they're still under the ground. Clever scanning machines can show what lies deep underneath the surface of

fossils without needing to break them open. Special lasers can create detailed maps of fragile fossil bones. Powerful microscopes help scientists see really tiny individual cells in well-preserved fossils. And computers can produce virtual models showing what God's dinosaurs might have looked like and even how they might have moved.

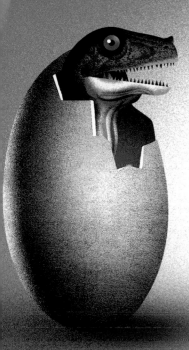

NEW DISCOVERIES

Fascinating new fossils tell us more and more about God's incredible dinosaurs.

In 2020, scientists reported the discovery of the first 3D fossil of a sauropod still inside its egg! A special scan of this tiny fossil showed an **egg tooth**–like structure on the end of its nose, just like many baby birds have today to break out of their eggshells.

Also in 2020, scientists found a tiny, 99-million-year-old skull preserved in amber (fossilized tree sap). With a jaw full of sharp little teeth, scientists named the creature *Oculudentavis* [OCK-you-luh-DENT-ah-viss] and suggested that it was the smallest dinosaur yet discovered. But since then, other scientists have suggested that it might be an ancient lizard-like reptile and not a dinosaur at all.

[God said] "I am putting you in charge of the fish, the birds, and all the wild animals." Genesis 1:28 TLB

EXPLORING GOD'S WORLD

We can learn so much about God from his creation as well as the Bible. His processes leave us lots of clues about how he creates, even in the rocks! And God loves to see us using his gift of science to explore and find out about all that he has made.

The Bible tells us that God asks his children (that's us!) to care for the world and its creatures. Finding out about ancient creatures like dinosaurs shows us the spectacular diversity of God's creation throughout history, and also how much our fragile Earth environments can change. The more we learn about all that God has created, the more we can be reminded of God's love for his creation and our responsibility to care for it.

The Earth has been wonderfully put together by a loving Creator. So let's take good care of it, explore, and discover even more about God's incredible creation!

Who knows what other amazing clues we'll find that tell us about the animals that roamed God's creation long, long ago. Maybe you'll be one of the paleontologists who finds out more!

GLOSSARY

A

Atmosphere The protective blanket or layer of gas around the Earth, including oxygen and carbon dioxide, which are important for life.

B

Bacteria Tiny organisms, each made of only one cell, which are found almost everywhere on Earth, including in and on you. Some bacteria are helpful, and some are harmful.

Bible The holy book of the Christian faith, containing a collection of separate books that form the main ideas Christians believe.

Big Bang The name given to the best current scientific understanding of how the universe began.

C

Christian A person who believes that Jesus is the son of God, who died and rose from the dead so that everyone can know God fully, and who lives according to the Bible.

Climate Long-term general weather conditions of an area or the whole world.

Convergent evolution When two or more species, not closely related, separately evolve similar characteristics.

Creation The universe, or everything that God has made. The process of God making everything.

D

Descendants The children, grandchildren, great-grandchildren, and so on of a living thing. For example, you are a descendant of your parents, grandparents, great-great-great-great-grandparents . . .

E

Egg tooth A hard growth on the beak or nose of birds and some other animals, used to help them break out through the shell when hatching.

Environment All the living and non-living things in a particular area, or the whole world, from rocks, soil, air, and water to plants and animals.

Evolution The process of change by which life on earth has become more and more different over time.

G

Generation A step in the growth of a family: great-grandparents, grandparents, parents, and children are each part of a different generation.

Geologist A scientist who studies the planet and its processes, including rocks, volcanoes, and earthquakes.

I

Invertebrates Animals that do not have a backbone, such as worms and insects.

J

Jesus Christians believe that God is three "persons" in one: the Father, the Son (Jesus), and the Holy Spirit. The Bible teaches that Jesus came to the Earth, lived and died as a human, and came back to life again, so that people could know God fully.

M

Microscope A tool used for making very tiny things look bigger so that we can study them.

Microscopic Something so tiny that we need a microscope to see it properly.

Minister, pastor, priest, reverend, vicar Titles given to church leaders.

Mummy Dead creature whose remains have been preserved in a special way that stops its soft parts from rotting away.

N

Nutrients Certain kinds of chemicals that living things are made of and need to eat to stay alive.

O

Organism A scientific name meaning "living thing," which includes bacteria, plants, and animals.

P

Predator An animal that hunts and eats other animals.

Preserved Stopped from rotting away, disappearing from Earth, or being destroyed.

R

Radiation The movement of particles or waves of energy, such as visible light or X-rays. Some forms of radiation can be detected with special tools like Geiger counters.

S

Specimen A specific animal, plant, or rock that we can study to learn more about it and others like it.

V

Vertebrates Animals with a spine (backbone), such as fish, amphibians, and mammals.

X

X-rays A type of electromagnetic radiation, a bit like light, which can be used to make images of the insides of fossils.

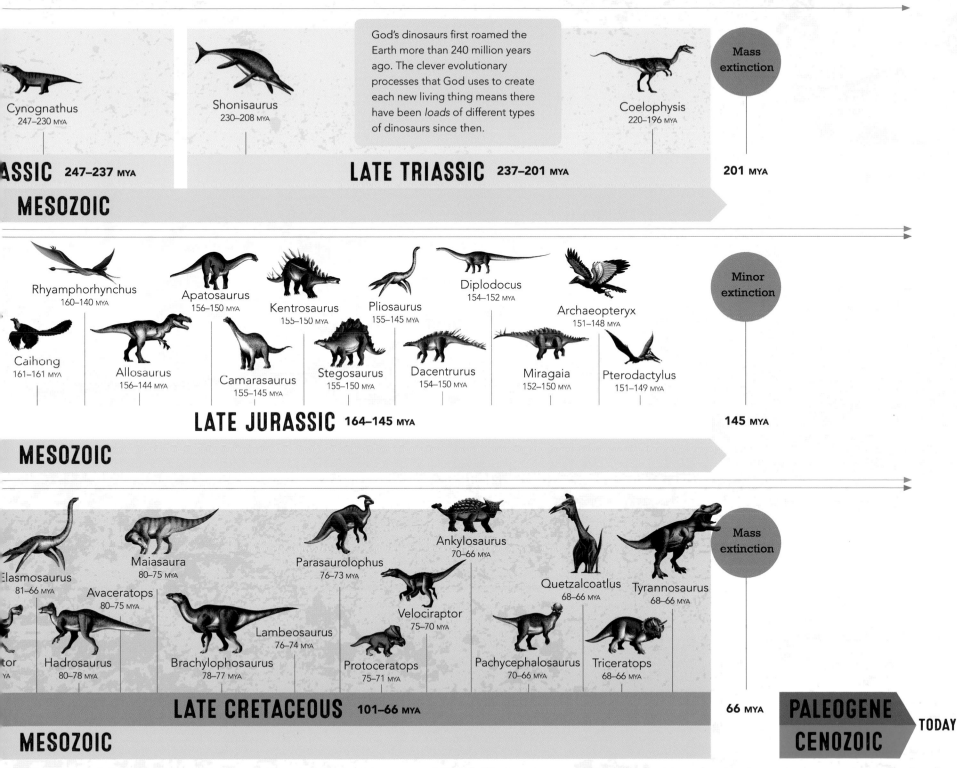

Cynognathus
247–230 MYA

Shonisaurus
230–208 MYA

God's dinosaurs first roamed the Earth more than 240 million years ago. The clever evolutionary processes that God uses to create each new living thing means there have been *loads* of different types of dinosaurs since then.

Coelophysis
220–196 MYA

Mass extinction

ASSIC 247–237 MYA

LATE TRIASSIC 237–201 MYA

201 MYA

MESOZOIC

Rhyamphorhynchus
160–140 MYA

Apatosaurus
156–150 MYA

Kentrosaurus
155–150 MYA

Pliosaurus
155–145 MYA

Diplodocus
154–152 MYA

Archaeopteryx
151–148 MYA

Minor extinction

Caihong
161–161 MYA

Allosaurus
156–144 MYA

Camarasaurus
155–145 MYA

Stegosaurus
155–150 MYA

Dacentrurus
154–150 MYA

Miragaia
152–150 MYA

Pterodactylus
151–149 MYA

LATE JURASSIC 164–145 MYA

145 MYA

MESOZOIC

Elasmosaurus
81–66 MYA

Maiasaura
80–75 MYA

Avaceratops
80–75 MYA

Parasaurolophus
76–73 MYA

Ankylosaurus
70–66 MYA

Quetzalcoatlus
68–66 MYA

Tyrannosaurus
68–66 MYA

Mass extinction

...tor
...YA

Hadrosaurus
80–78 MYA

Brachylophosaurus
78–77 MYA

Lambeosaurus
76–74 MYA

Protoceratops
75–71 MYA

Velociraptor
75–70 MYA

Pachycephalosaurus
70–66 MYA

Triceratops
68–66 MYA

LATE CRETACEOUS 101–66 MYA

66 MYA

PALEOGENE

TODAY

MESOZOIC

CENOZOIC

MYA = million years ago   Dinosaurs not to scale

Learn more about dinosaurs and be amazed at everything God made!

From the mighty T. rex to the speedy velociraptor, explore the wide range of incredible dinosaurs God created. Each page is packed with prehistoric facts and bright, detailed illustrations that describe what we know about these amazing creatures and the ways God crafted them to live in his world. You'll also learn about fossils and genetics, and hear from Christian paleontologists and scientists who show how God designed faith and science to work together to uncover the secrets of his creation.

So dig in and start discovering!

The
Faraday
Institute
for Science and Religion

ZONDERkidz™
.com

USD $14.99 / CAD $18.50
ISBN 978-0-310-14471-7

51499

9 780310 144717

Printed in Korea